# Bowling

# Contents

When using this book, concentrate on one coaching point at a time. Practise each point until you are happy you have mastered it before moving on to the next one.

Sri Lankan bowler Lasith Malinga combines great pace with swing.

# INTRODUCTION

There are many different types of bowlers, from electrifying pacemen who bowl at 90 miles an hour, such as Australia's Brett Lee, to wily spin bowlers like Sri Lanka's Muttiah Muralitharan, and clever seam and swing bowlers like England one-day star James Anderson. Whichever kind of bowler you want to be, this book will help you to improve.

In this book we look at the key skills needed to be a top bowler. Bowling fast, spinning the ball or making it swing are not enough on their own. You must also have great accuracy and control, to build pressure on the batsman and force him to make a mistake.

## WHAT MAKES A GOOD BOWLER?

- Accuracy
- Consistency
- Movement: seam, swing or spin
- Athleticism
- Control
- Patience
- Intelligence to work out a batsman's weakness
- Stamina
- Variation

Top bowlers can come in many different shapes, styles and sizes but they all have a number of important skills in common. Most wickets are taken by bowling a number of good balls in a row and causing the batsman to make a mistake rather than by a 'magic' delivery. It's no good bowling a great ball every now and then if the other balls are bad.

Good bowlers should have the ability to vary their bowling and keep the batsmen guessing. It is a good idea to have several types of delivery in your armoury to help you take wickets. England's James Anderson is able to bowl away-swingers and in-swingers as well as varying his pace and the length he bowls. These variations mean a batsman cannot afford to lose concentration for a second.

A top-class bowler also needs to be physically fit. Fast bowlers must be athletic to avoid injury while spinners must be able to field well off their own bowling to save runs and take catches. Bowlers also need good stamina as they may be required to bowl a lot of overs in a day.

Successful bowlers will be able to work out a batsman's weaknesses and test them out with seam, swing or spin.

England's Andrew Flintoff is a master at building pressure by bowling well, ball after ball.

**DID YOU KNOW?**

Sri Lanka's Lasith Malinga is the first bowler to take four wickets in successive balls in an International match. He performed the feat against South Africa in the 2007 World Cup.

# BOWLING TO A **PLAN**

A bowler has two main roles. One is to take wickets and the other is to stop the batsman from scoring runs. Often these two roles go hand in hand, as stopping the batsman scoring puts him under pressure and can force him into making a mistake. Occasionally you may take a wicket with an unplayable delivery, but more commonly a wicket will come about through a batsman's error after a prolonged spell of good bowling.

A basic game plan for any young bowler should focus on developing a 'stock' ball (see page 6), which you can repeat over and over again, and bowling a consistent line and length. It takes patience and practice to bowl consistently but once you have mastered this control you will be a tough opponent.

## LINE

Line refers to the direction of your delivery. A good line for most bowlers will be on or just outside off-stump. This is a difficult line for batsmen, as they are unsure whether to leave the ball or play a shot.

 To bowl a good line and length it is vital to keep your eyes on the target.

- If you are bowling in swing or off spin your ideal line will be just outside off-stump to allow the ball to move back into the batsman.
- If you are bowling away swing, a good line is off-stump, or in between middle and off, to allow for movement away from the batsman.
- Leg-spinners should start by bowling the ball in line with middle-stump or between middle and off, so the ball will spin to off-stump or just outside.
- The line you bowl will be affected by the amount the ball swings, seams or spins. Avoid bowling on or outside leg-stump or you will make it easy for the batsman to score runs.

## LENGTH

Length refers to the area of the pitch where the ball bounces. For a guide to the different lengths bowlers use, see the diagram opposite.

Most bowlers should look to bowl in the area shown as a good length on the pitch map. This will make the batsman play off the front foot. Often a batsman will be unsure whether to attack or

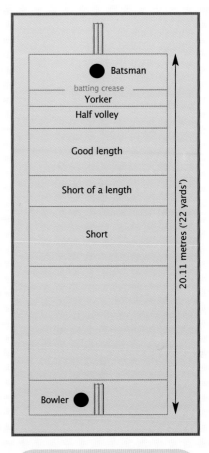

This map is intended as a guide to bowling length. Actual lengths will vary depending on the type of bowler you are. For example, a good length for a spinner will be fuller than for a quicker bowler.

full length is vital for quick bowlers in order for the ball to swing. It is also crucial for spinners as the batsman has less time to react to the spinning ball, which makes it much harder to play.

The pitch map diagram on page 5 is a useful guideline for length, though the length you bowl may vary depending on the pace and bounce of the wicket you are playing on.

## STOCK BALL

The stock ball is mentioned quite a lot in this book. It simply refers to a bowler's most common delivery. For example, an off-spinner's stock ball is the off-break. It is vital that every player develops their stock ball before attempting variations. A reliable stock ball of good line and length is the most important ball for any bowler and should be the base from which you learn and develop new skills.

## PRE-MATCH PREPARATION

It is vital that all young bowlers warm up properly before they bowl, either in a match or training session. This should be

A spinnner should try to make his stock ball turn as much as possible.

defend a good length delivery and this can lead to a wicket-taking opportunity. A good length delivery gives the bowler a chance of every mode of dismissal from bowled to LBW to be caught, whereas short-pitched bowling removes the chance of bowled or LBW as the ball will bounce higher than the stumps. Good players will punish short-pitched bowling and score freely from it. While learning their trade it is better for young bowlers to forget about bowling short until they are older and fully developed. Bowling a organised by your coach as part of a team warm-up, but there may be occasions when you have to do some extra preparation yourself.

## STRETCHING

It is important to do a number of stretches before you bowl, concentrating on your back, arms and major leg muscles. Stretching will help you avoid injury and also make sure you are loose and ready to bowl when the game starts.

## Practice

This simple drill for target bowling should be done before a game but can also be done during practice sessions.

- Place cones down on a good line and length as a target.
- Attempt to bowl the ball into the target as often as possible. This should be done without a batsman.
- Repeat this exercise until you feel confident you can bowl the ball in the right area consistently.
- If you are practising before a game, it is important not to tire yourself out.

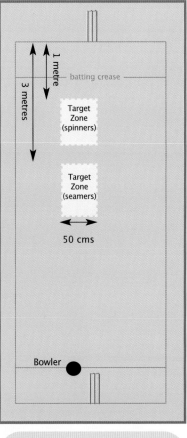

1 metre

3 metres

batting crease

Target Zone (spinners)

Target Zone (seamers)

50 cms

Bowler

Set up your target zone about half-a-metre wide, with the inside in line with middle-stump.

# BOWLING **ACTIONS**

If you watch top bowlers on TV you will notice that no two bowlers bowl in exactly the same way. Each has a slightly different natural action, though it must fall into one of the three categories of fast bowling actions: side-on, front-on or mid-way.

No one type of action is 'better' than another. Side-on is the most commonly taught, but the important thing is to bowl with the action that feels most natural to you. To avoid injury you should ensure that your feet, hips and shoulders are all aligned.

## SIDE-ON

Side-on is the classic fast-bowling action, practised by stars such as England's James Anderson and Matthew Hoggard.

## COACHING POINTS

- When bowling side-on your back foot should be parallel to the crease and your front foot pointing at the target.
- Hips and shoulders must be side-on to your target.
- Your head should look just outside your front arm.

England's Matthew Hoggard is a good example of a bowler with a side-on action.

With a front-on action the chest is open in the delivery stride.

Side-on is the best action to produce away swing (see pages 19 and 20). Most young bowlers will be taught to bowl side-on as this action is more effective for a developing body. However, if you normally bowl front-on or mid-way, you should not change your action.

## FRONT-ON

The front-on bowling action is used by a number of top bowlers, including West Indies all-rounder Dwayne Bravo and England's Steve Harmison.

## COACHING POINTS

- When bowling front-on both feet should point down the wicket.
- Your hips and shoulders should point across the wicket leaving you chest-on to the target.
- You should look at the target from inside your front arm.
- Make sure you keep your shoulders front-on throughout the action.

Front-on bowlers are usually best suited to bowling in swing.

A young bowler with a mid-way action. Note the similarity to Test star Brett Lee, opposite.

## MID-WAY

Australian fast bowler Brett Lee is a good example of a bowler with a mid-way action. It is a compromise between side-on and front-on and can also be called a 45-degree action due to the angle of alignment of feet, hips and shoulders.

## COACHING POINTS

- In a mid-way action the feet, hips and shoulders should point at a 45-degree angle at the time the back foot lands.
- The eyes should be looking directly through the front arm towards the target.

Mid-way actions often suit taller bowlers as they help provide stability at the crease and cut down on twisting that could cause injury.

### SAFE TECHNIQUE

Research by top sports scientists found that bowlers with side-on, front-on and mid-way actions were less at risk from injury than those with mixed actions, where shoulders, hips and feet are unaligned. If you are concerned you may have a mixed action, or experience pain when bowling, get a qualified coach to observe you.

Australia's Brett Lee in full cry. His extreme pace has made him one of the most feared bowlers in Test cricket.

# BREAKING IT **DOWN**

**B**owling is a complex skill made up of several key phases, and it is easier to work on your action when you break it down.

A smooth and controlled run-up is vital to every bowler.

## THE RUN-UP

All bowling actions start with the run-up, which will vary in length, speed and angle depending on the type of bowler you are. Whether you have a long, sprint-style run-up like India's Sreesanth or a slower more controlled approach like England's Simon Jones, many of the key points remain the same.

A good run-up should be:

* **Smooth and rhythmical**. Your strides should be comfortable and of equal length. There should be a gentle acceleration through your run-up, so you are at your fastest just before you take off into the 'bound'.

* **Balanced.** You should remain balanced with your head in an upright position throughout. Keep your eyes focused on a point on the pitch or on the stumps as you run in to help keep your head still.

* **Consistent:** Your run-up must be consistent and repeatable. It

should be identical every time you bowl, so that you don't over-step the line and bowl a no-ball.

## WHAT IS A NO-BALL?

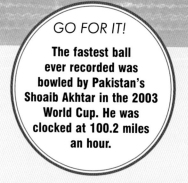

For a ball to be legal the bowler must have part of his front foot behind the bowling crease. If your heel is on or over the line it is a no-ball, which means a batsman can score runs from it, but you can't take a wicket. The ball must then be bowled again. A no-ball is also called if any part of the bowler's back foot is outside the side-line of the crease.

To ensure you don't bowl a no-ball you must have a repeatable run-up you can produce every single time you bowl. Even top international bowlers get it wrong sometimes, but here are a few tips to help.

### Common fault

Many young fast bowlers try to sprint in too fast. Run-up is all about rhythm, not speed. You don't want to run in like a 100-metre sprinter.

### Practice

When attempting to find your run-up, start by doing it in reverse.

- Place the heel of your starting foot on the front crease line and perform your run-up running away from the wicket.

- Bowl a delivery at a point which feels comfortable, and have someone to mark where the toe of your front foot lands at the point of delivery.

- When you have done this try to recreate the run-up in the proper direction, with your friend watching where your front foot lands.

- Start your run-up with the same foot each time and ensure that the toe of your starting foot is just behind your bowling mark.

- Repeat the exercise until you are confident you can bowl consistently without no-balling. When you can do this, measure your run-up with a tape measure or normal walking paces so that you can recreate it wherever you play.

The bound, which is sometimes referred to as the jump and gather.

# THE BOUND

This phase of the bowling action involves jumping up and landing at the end of your run-up. Many young bowlers find it difficult working out which foot they should take off and land on.

- A right-arm bowler should take off on his left foot and land on his right foot.
- For a left-armer the reverse is true.
- When you land, your back foot must be pointing in the correct direction for your bowling action. This will mean some rotation of the body in mid-air for side-on bowlers.

## Common fault

Many young bowlers naturally take off and land on the same foot. This stops the action being smooth and generating pace. These drills will help you solve the problem, but it may take some time until it feels natural to bowl off the correct foot.

## Practice

Initially you should walk through the bowling action rather than running in.

- Stamp your take-off foot on the ground before walking through each delivery, so it tingles slightly, or roll up your trouser leg. This will help you indentify the take-off foot.
- Walk through your bowling action without attempting to jump, making sure that your feet move in the correct sequence.
- If you are right-handed the sequence will be:
  - Take off on left foot.
  - Land on right foot.
  - Bowl from left foot.

  Say the words of the sequence in your head as you do it – "left, right, left."
- When you can perform that drill comfortably, mark a line halfway between the point of take-off and landing and place a small obstacle, such as a line of cones, in the way.
- Walk through the action with your feet in the correct sequence ensuring you do not tread on the obstacle.
- Next, try to jump over the obstacle still using the correct sequence of feet.
- When you have done this drill enough times for it to feel natural then you can start to attempt it with a run-up and a ball in your hand.

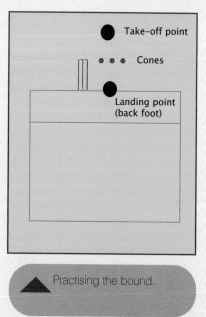

Take-off point

Cones

Landing point (back foot)

Practising the bound.

- You may need to do this a large number of times before it feels natural. The younger you are, the easier it will be to change. It may take older players a bit longer to adjust.

## BE THE BEST

Imagine you are enclosed in a glass box. Both arms should remain inside the box through the coil phase of delivery. If your arms go too wide of your body you will lose rhythm and balance. All your energy should be pushing towards your target.

## THE COIL

The coil phase of the action is between landing at the bowling crease and releasing the ball. Your position will differ slightly depending on which type of action you have, but there are some common points.

## COACHING POINTS

- Stay as tall and balanced as you can with your head still and eyes level looking at the target.
- Keep your front arm high so your elbow is higher than your shoulder.
- Your bowling arm should remain close to your body.
- Your feet hips and shoulders should be aligned for your type of action.
- Try to land close to the stumps.

## THE RELEASE

- At the point of release make sure you are balanced, with head still, looking at the target.
- Your bowling arm should be at

The coil

The release

about 11 o'clock, with your wrist behind the ball.

- Pull your non-bowling arm through, past your front hip and drive your back leg towards the target.

# THE FOLLOW-THROUGH

The follow-through comes after you have released the ball. It is a key part of the bowling action which can often be forgotten.

# COACHING POINTS

- Your follow-through should be powerful with a full swing of your arms and your back leg driving through.

- It should help you continue your journey down the wicket towards your target.

- You should keep your head and eyes up looking at the target and stop running naturally rather than by consciously 'pulling up'.

Watch top fast bowlers on television and notice how far down the wicket they follow through. You are not allowed to run on the pitch, so try to follow through at a slight angle away from it.

## Practice

- To practise your follow-through simply create a 'corridor' of cones from the bowling crease through to the end of your follow-through. The cones should take you away from the pitch at a very gentle angle (see diagram below).

- At first, just walk for a few strides before bowling, then drive your body down the path of cones after releasing the ball and allow your natural momentum to take you through. You should be able to stay in the line of cones.

- Continue this drill by building in your full run-up. The practice will also help keep all your energy towards the target, making you a more efficient, faster bowler.

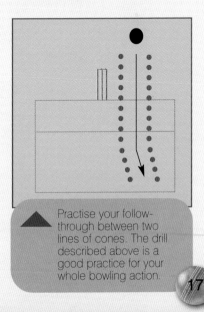

Practise your follow-through between two lines of cones. The drill described above is a good practice for your whole bowling action.

17

## Common fault

Young bowlers often fall away, and follow through on a sharp angle towards the off-side. This is usually caused by being unbalanced at the crease and can lead to the ball going down the leg-side. Keep your head up and eyes level as you release the ball to help you follow through towards your target.

### BE THE BEST

Choose a place to look at as you bowl, such as the top of the off-stump, and stay focused on it from the start of your action through to the completion of your follow-through. This will help keep you balanced and bowl more accurately. If you find that this makes you bowl too full, simply lower your gaze to the middle or bottom of off-stump and you should bowl a slightly shorter length.

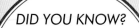

Keep your eyes on the target as you follow through, driving your right arm past your left hip.

### DID YOU KNOW?

England's highest ever Test wicket-taker is Ian Botham, who claimed 383 victims in a fantastic career as an all-rounder.

# SWING **BOWLING**

Swing is a key weapon in the armoury of a fast bowler, and causes the ball to move into or away from the batsman as it travels towards him. It is caused by a combination of the way the bowler grips the ball, and his bowling action.

The amount a ball swings depends on many different factors; the skill of the bowler, the state of the ball, the weather, and can even be affected by the tide and the number of trees around a ground!

For a ball to swing it should have a shiny side and a slightly scuffed side. This is why you see cricketers shining the ball against their trousers. If you look closely you will notice they only shine one side of the ball. If the ball is released with a vertical seam, it should swing in the direction of the scuffed side of the ball.

There are two types of swing, in swing and out swing. Generally side-on bowlers find it easier to bowl out swing and front-on bowlers are more suited to in swing. However, top bowlers are able to swing the ball both ways without changing their action.

England's James Anderson can swing the ball both ways.

## OUT SWING

If a right-arm bowler bowls an away-swinger to a right-handed batsman, the ball will move in the air towards the off-side.

### Grip

- Have your first two fingers either side of the seam with the side of your thumb on the seam underneath the ball.
- Keep the ball towards the end of the fingers.
- The scuffed side of the ball should be on the left and the seam slightly angled towards the off-side.

## IN SWING

If a right-arm bowler bowls an in swinger to a right-handed

batsman, the ball will move in the air towards the leg-side.

### Grip

- Grip the ball with your first two fingers close together either side of the seam with the flat part of your thumb on the seam underneath the ball.
- The scuffed side should be on the right with the seam slightly angled towards the leg-side.

To bowl in swing, the scuffed side of the ball should be on the left.

To bowl out swing, the scuffed side should be on the right.

# SEAM **BOWLING**

The second major weapon for any fast bowler is seam movement. This occurs when the seam of the ball hits the pitch at an angle, which makes the ball deviate after bouncing. It is difficult for batsmen to play against because they have little time to react. England's Andrew Flintoff is a good example of a bowler who makes great use of seam movement.

A ball will seam from the same grips used for swing bowling. The only adjustment a seam bowler may make is to bowl the ball slightly shorter.

The key for all young fast bowlers is to release the ball with the seam upright and the wrist and fingers behind the ball.

## VARIATIONS

The main aim for any young bowler should be to bowl good line and length consistently, and to reproduce his stock ball at will. Once you have mastered this you should try to develop variations, which will keep batsmen guessing and test them out in different ways. Here are several variations you can try.

A good wrist position is important if you want the ball to seam or swing.

# THE YORKER

Every great fast bowler is able to bowl a good yorker. This is a ball which is really full in length and pitches by the batsman's feet. It is an awkward length for batsmen to play, and it can sneak under the bat to hit the stumps. The yorker is often bowled slightly quicker than a bowler's normal delivery which adds to the element of surprise.

## Practice

- Place a square of cones on the pitch just in front of where the batsman would normally stand.
- Practise trying to bowl the ball into this target area.
- You could do this practice with your friends and keep score to make it competitive.

- Award points for landing the ball in the target and extra points if the ball goes on to hit the wickets.
- Start with the target fairly wide and make it gradually smaller so it ends up being only the width of the wickets.
- The most important thing to concentrate on is the length. Once you have mastered this you can start to practise bowling the correct line.
- Refer to the pitch map on page 5.

## Next step

Remove the cones and replace the stumps with a target half as high, such as a plastic milk-crate. If you bowl a yorker it will hit the target but any ball that is shorter in length will fly over the top. This will help you get your length just right.

## SLOWER BALLS

Every top bowler is able to vary his pace, and a well-disguised slower ball can often make the batsman play too early and hit it in the air for a catching opportunity. There are a number of different ways to bowl a slower ball. The secret of a good slower ball is to bowl it with the same action and arm speed as normal but for the ball to come out slowly. Here is one version to try.

- Hold the ball as you would for a normal delivery, with one finger either side of the seam and thumb on the bottom.

### BE THE BEST

These small changes will make the ball come out slightly slower. They may also make the ball drop slightly shorter, so make sure you aim to bowl a fuller length than usual to compensate.

- Now push the ball right back into the hand so you are practically holding it in your palm.
- Squeeze the ball tighter than usual.
- There are several different types of slower ball. This is just one example.

Notice how the ball is held much further back in the hand than normal. It won't come out 'super slow' but the change of pace should be enough to surprise the batsman.

# CUTTERS

Some bowlers use cutters as variations to their stock ball. They are bowled by rolling the fingers over the seam, and by the seam hitting the pitch at an acute angle.

## The off cutter

The off cutter will deviate in towards a right-handed batsman from off to leg after bouncing. It is often used as a variation delivery by an away-swing bowler as it moves the opposite way to an away-swinger but can be bowled without making any major adjustment to your action. The movement is caused by rotation imparted on the ball at the point of release.

- Grip the ball with your first finger along the seam and the side of your thumb on the bottom.
- Lower your second finger until it is about a third of the way down the side of the ball facing the leg-side.
- As you release the ball, turn your wrist clockwise like turning a door handle, running your fingers down the side of the ball which faces the leg-side.

## The leg cutter

The leg cutter moves away from a right-handed batsman after bouncing and is a good variation for an in swing bowler. Like the off cutter, it requires plenty of practice before being attempted in a game.

- Grip the ball with your second finger running down the seam and your thumb on the bottom.
- Slide your second finger just off the seam on the side of the ball facing the off-side.
- On release, slightly turn your wrist anti-clockwise so you run your fingers down the side of the ball facing the off-side.

Grip for the off cutter, then flick your wrist clockwise.

Grip for the leg cutter. In this case, flick your wrist anti-clockwise.

# SPIN **BOWLING**

The two highest Test wicket-takers of all time are spinners – Australian leg-spinner Shane Warne and Sri Lankan off-spinner Muttiah Muralitharan have both taken over 700 Test wickets. They are masters of the art of spin bowling and have bamboozled, confused and confounded batsman around the world. The secret of their success is their ability to combine big spin, deceptive variation and incredible control. This combination of skills is the key for all spinners, whether they are off-spinners, leg-spinners or left-arm spinners such as England's Monty Panesar.

## OFF SPIN

An off-spinner uses his fingers to make the ball spin into a right-handed batsman from off-side to leg-side. Grip the ball with the first two fingers, with the first joints of these fingers spread widely on the seam. The thumb should not be in contact with the ball. Spin is imparted mainly by the first finger and through turning your wrist clockwise as though opening a door.

### Practice

• If you are new to spin, practise releasing the ball as above and simply throwing it to a partner 5 or 10 metres away, allowing the ball to bounce once.

Off spin is also known as finger spin, as it uses the index and middle fingers to spin the ball.

## BE THE BEST

Carry a ball round with you and practise spinning it from your bowling hand and catching it in the other. You could do this whenever you have a spare moment, such as when watching TV or waiting for a bus. The more you do it the more natural it will feel when you bowl.

## BOWLING FROM THE COIL

Before attempting to bowl from a full run-up, practise bowling from the coil phase of the action. Here are some points to help you.

- Start with your back foot parallel to the crease. Look behind your front arm and keep your head up and still.

- Your delivery stride should be short and slightly angled. At the point of release you should stand tall with your bowling arm up at 11 o'clock.

- Place your weight on the ball of your front foot and pivot so that the right knee drives through towards the target. Keep your head up and still throughout.

- Watch the ball carefully and see if you notice it rotating through the air and deviating off the pitch after it lands.

- Young bowlers should try to impart as much spin on the ball as possible; control can be learned later on.

The approach. Keep it balanced and rhythmical.

The coil. A strong front arm will improve accuracy.

- In the follow-through your body pivots 180 degrees so that your back leg is now nearest the batsman. Your head should still be held high, and you should still be looking at the batsman.
- When you feel confident bowling from the coil, start to work on your run-up. A spinner's run-up will be shorter than a seamer's but still needs to be smooth, rhythmical and repeatable. Try and remain light on your feet during your approach as this will help you move smoothly through the action.

## Common fault

Many young bowlers fail to pivot

on their front leg and they follow through like a seamer instead. Pivoting helps you impart more spin on the ball as your body works with your fingers to make the ball turn.

It is vital to keep your head up and eyes level throughout the action to keep you balanced. After completing the pivot you should be in a position to collect the ball should the batsman hit it back at you.

The release. Remember to pivot on the ball of your front foot.

The follow-through. The body completes a 180-degree pivot.

# LEG SPIN

Leg spin is also referred to as wrist spin, as the bowler uses his wrist in combination with his fingers and body to impart spin on the ball. A leg spin delivery will move away from a right-handed batsman, from leg to off, after bouncing. Leg spin will usually turn more than off spin, but is harder to control.

Shane Warne stood out from other leg-spinners as he rarely bowled a bad ball and was able to build pressure on the batsmen. Young spinners should concentrate on getting the ball to spin. Control can be improved later on.

Leg spin grip

## Practice

Practise releasing the ball by working with a partner and throwing it underarm. Stand facing your partner, bring your bowling arm back past your hips, palm facing forward. As you bring your arm forward flick your wrist

## Grip

- The top joints of the first two fingers lie across the seam with the third finger bent along the seam. The thumb should remain off the ball.

- Spin is imparted by the third finger and a flick of the wrist. You should flick your wrist anti-clockwise so the ball is released from the back of the hand.

The approach

The coil

**3** The release

**4** The follow-through

so that your palm ends up facing the ground. You should be able to see the ball rotating through the air and deviating off the pitch. When you feel confident releasing the ball underarm, try bowling from the coil.

- Start in a side-on position, back foot parallel to the crease, looking behind the front arm. Keep your head up and eyes level.

- Your delivery stride will be a little longer than for off spin and angled slightly towards the leg-side. Keep your head up and still.

- At the point of release stand tall with your arm at 11 o'clock. Pivot on the ball of your front

foot and drive your back leg through. Maintain an upright, steady head position.

- Your follow-through should be powerful and energetic with a full swing of the arms. Your back leg should come through so that your right hip is nearest the batsman. Your head should still be upright looking at the batsman.

## Common fault

Many young leg-spinners fall away to the off-side during delivery as they try to put big spin on the ball. This will make the ball go down leg-side or be released as a full toss. Stay tall. Keep your head up throughout the action.

## LEFT-ARM SPIN

The same coaching points for off spin also apply to orthodox left-arm spin. The only difference is that you will bowl from a different angle and the ball will move from leg to off, away from a right-handed batsman. Make sure your feet, hips and shoulders are aligned and point in line with where you want to pitch the ball. Top left-arm spinners alter the angle of their bowling and are comfortable bowling over or around the wicket.

Left-arm wrist spinners are like leg-spinners in reverse, moving the ball from off to leg to the right-handed batsman. This delivery is known as a Chinaman.

### Practice

A good practice for all types of spinner is to bowl with a set of stumps two-thirds of the way down the wicket. Try to make the ball bounce beyond them. This will help you to flight the ball.

A left-arm wrist spinner delivers a Chinaman.

The whole body should be used in the follow-through.

# SPIN **VARIATIONS**

Top spin bowlers are not only able to bowl a good stock ball but they can also deceive the batsman through a number of variation deliveries. Young spinners should be able to consistently bowl their stock ball before attempting to master a variation, but here are tips on how to bowl the floater, which should be used as a variation to the off-break, and the googly, which is a variation to the leg-break.

## THE FLOATER

Instead of spinning from off to leg after pitching, the floater moves through the air from leg to off. This is caused by presenting the seam as for an out-swinger at the point of delivery. The finger position pictured enables the ball to be released like an out-swinger, deceiving the batsman into playing as though the ball is an offbreak. Instead it will move in the opposite direction, which may cause the batsman to miss or edge the ball.

### GO FOR IT!

**This ball shows that spinners can use swing to good effect as well as quick bowlers. Make sure you look after the ball and keep shining one side as it will benefit your bowling.**

## THE GOOGLY

The googly is a ball which spins from off to leg while appearing to be a leg-break. When bowled well this ball completely deceives batsmen. It can be very hard to distinguish the googly from the leg-break until after the ball has pitched. The movement is caused by over-rotating the wrist during the release. The ball is released with

This is the grip for the floater. Present the ball seam up.

the same grip as for the leg-spinner but is released from the very back of the hand.

## OTHER VARIATIONS

There are a number of other ways to add variation to your bowling. You should practice bowling from close to the stumps and wide on the crease to change your angle of delivery. Just a simple change of angle can often deceive a batsman. It is also useful to learn to bowl both over and around the wicket to vary the angle. Every bowler should have a stock delivery position and only need to vary it occasionally to surprise the batsman. Top spinners also use subtle changes in their flight and pace of delivery to test the batsman.

**BE THE BEST**

Remember to change the line of your delivery when bowling the googly. You need to start the ball outside off-stump for it to be effective. If you start the ball too straight it will spin down the leg-side making it easy for the batsman to score runs.

## THE LAST WORD

Bowling is a difficult skill to master, and you won't become a world-beater overnight, but the tips and practices in this book will help you to keep improving. The better you get, the more you will enjoy your cricket.

Notice how this left-arm wrist-spinner comes around the wicket to change his angle of attack.